KIDS SAY

DON'T SMOKE

POSTERS FROM THE SMOKE-FREE CONTEST

TEXT BY ANDREW TOBIAS

WORKMAN PUBLISHING • NEW YORK

ACKNOWLEDGMENTS

A great many people deserve thanks for this book, but let me mention just these few: Peter Workman, who quickly agreed to publish it; Sally Kovalchick and her colleagues, who brought the book to fruition; Joe Tye, whose *Tobacco & Youth Reporter* was the source of much of this research; and Tony Schwartz, Ed Koch, Stephen Joseph and Laurent Seitz, who are among the dozens of people who gave their time and talent to make the Smoke-Free Ad Contest a smashing success.

Library of Congress Cataloging-in-Publication Data
Kids say don't smoke: posters from the New York City Pro-Health Ad contest/ sponsored by Smokefree Educational Services: text by Andrew Tobias.

p. cm. ISBN 0-89480-998-9 (pbk.)
1. Smoking—New York (N.Y.)—Prevention. 2. Tobacco habit— New York (N.Y.)—Prevention. 3. Advertising, Public service—New York (N.Y.)
I. Tobias, Andrew P. II. Smokefree Educational Services (New York, N.Y.)
HV5768.N5K54 1991   90-50950
362.29'67'097471—dc20   CIP

Cover and book design by Susan Reinhardt
Title page poster: Stephanie Gregg, John Dewey High School, Brooklyn

Workman Publishing Company, Inc.
708 Broadway
New York, New York 10003

Manufactured in the United States of America
First Printing April 1991
10 9 8 7 6 5 4 3 2

Cynthia Vera,
P.S. 63, Manhattan

SPREAD THE WORD

▼

All the ads in this book were done by kids for the New York City Smoke-Free Ad Contest. Kids like:

●Fourteen-year-old Stephanie Gregg, whose ad was turned into a T-shirt;

●James Jackson and Nigel Ricketts, two 10-year-olds who submitted their ad as a rap song on cassette and Nigel got to perform it live on the *Today* show; and

●Melissa Antonow, a fifth-grader whose ad wound up in every subway car in New York. In fact, it made the NBC *Nightly News* twice, became the subject of a New York *Times* editorial and was shown by CNN all over the world.

In all, more than 100,000 entries came in from over 700 of the city's schools, each one saying in its own way: "Don't smoke." But to understand why the contest was such a success, you have to know something about Joe Cherner and his vision of a pro-health environment.

A BREATH OF FRESH AIR

Joseph W. Cherner was born in Washington, D.C., in 1958. In college, he traded rare coins. After college, he went to work on Wall Street. In his spare time, at the age of 28, he decided to take on the tobacco industry.

It wasn't that Joe was against *smokers,* or that he didn't feel sorry for them. He just hated having to breathe their smoke. Even more,

more, he hated to see kids become addicted to cigarettes. He knew they didn't realize what they were getting themselves into. Or what the cigarette companies were doing to manipulate them.

Determined to do something—because smoking kills more Americans each year than alcohol, fires, automobile accidents and AIDS combined—he put up $100,000 of his own money to sponsor a pro-health, smoke-free ad contest among New York City school kids.

He visited many of the schools himself, taking along celebrities like C. Everett Koop (former U.S. Surgeon General), Mets pitcher Ron Darling (whose dad used to carry a battery-powered fan into restaurants to blow smoke away) and Patrick Reynolds (who remembers his father, R.J. Reynolds Jr., lying on the floor with bags of sand on his chest, dying of emphysema).

The contest was a hit. Dozens of winners, ranging in age from 7 to 18, were presented with savings bonds at City Hall under the lights of local and national TV cameras. There were speeches. The Mayor came by to offer his congratulations. New York's Health Commissioner spoke. A man with no voice box described what it was like to have to breathe through a hole in his throat. (Smoking had given him cancer of the larynx; he spoke with the aid of a metal device held up to his throat.) It was a memorable afternoon.

Now, with the help of Scholastic Inc., Joe's smoke-free ad contest is going nationwide and to Canada. If your school isn't signed up to participate, have your principal contact *Scholastic* magazine for information on getting involved.

MISSION ALL-TOO-POSSIBLE

In the old days, tobacco companies handed out free cigarettes in schools—a highly effective way of hooking new customers. When that was finally outlawed, they retreated to handing out free cigarettes *near* schools and at rock concerts and in shopping malls. In 1990, Joe Cherner photographed Newport models giving free cigarettes to 10- and 11-year-olds. After seeing these photographs and hearing from health advocates, the New York City Council unanimously passed a ban on the free distribution of cigarettes.

But equally out of place are cigarette vending machines. These machines send a false message that cigarettes are as harmless as candy or soda pop. In addition, children who buy cigarettes from vending machines think they're getting around laws that prohibit cigarette sales to minors. They don't realize that one of the reasons cigarette vending machines exist is to get children addicted.

Tobacco companies and vendors pretend that children can't buy cigarettes from vending machines. (That's what they actually said before the New York City Council.) So health advocates uncovered documents from the vendors' own internal survey of 1,000 children showing that the younger a child is, the more likely he or she will use a vending machine to get cigarettes. Then Joe and six young friends, aged 11 to 15, conducted another survey. They visited all five boroughs of New York City to test 35 cigarette vending machines, chosen at random, located in:

Restaurants	11	Hotel	1
Bars	8	Video arcade	1
Pizza parlors	5	Ice-cream parlor	1
Supermarkets	4	Other	2
Bowling alleys	2		

In every case, the child who went to buy cigarettes did so easily. In almost all cases, the kids reported, adults watched them buy cigarettes but didn't care. On one occasion, a restaurant employee ran after an 11-year-old to tell him he'd forgotten his change. Joe's six young friends learned that all vendors really wanted from them was their money.

So, picture it! The tobacco industry and vending guys were telling the City Council it would be crazy to ban cigarette machines, especially from places like bars that were off-limits to minors . . . and then Joe and his friends dumped onto the hearing table piles of cigarettes the kids had bought in bars, unassisted, a few days before.

It was a great moment. And it led to the passage of a law that eliminates cigarette vending machines almost everywhere in New York City.

The kids won! After all, who was the City Council going to believe: a bunch of kids who had absolutely no reason to lie, or a bunch of cigarette representatives who are *paid* to lie? (Or do they really believe that it's not yet known whether smoking is bad for you?)

No other dangerous or cancer-causing product is sold through vending machines. Not switchblades, not firecrackers—not even beer. A growing number of cities have eliminated cigarette vending machines. Tomorrow's generation will wonder how we ever let tobacco companies trick children this way.

If your local town or city government hasn't banned the free distribution of cigarettes or cigarette vending machines, maybe you can use these examples, and some of the facts you'll find in this book, to help the adults who run things see reason. If it can be done in New York, it can be done almost anywhere.

A FEW PARTING PUFFS

Tobacco addiction kills 434,000 Americans each year. The only replacement smokers out there are children, because adults who don't smoke aren't going to start. We must stop tobacco companies from deceiving children into addiction. Cancer-causing, addictive drugs should be sold as such, with larger warnings to alert potential buyers. In addition, any U.S. cigarette company that fails to include warnings on cigarettes it sells abroad shouldn't be allowed to sell cigarettes in the United States. A pretty harsh point of view? You just might agree with it after you see what Marlboro country is really like.

This book is an inspiration to those who believe one young American *can* still make a difference, even against an adversary as entrenched and powerful as the tobacco industry. Royalties from its sale go to Smokefree Educational Services, Inc., the nonprofit organization Joe established and funded, and to which he volunteers his time.

**Erin Fels,
P.S. 52, Brooklyn**

One man chained himself to a 280-pound sofa for three weeks to quit smoking.

'll quit when I'm older." No—chances are you won't. Once you've started, it's hard to quit. And it gets harder and harder each month you wait. Smoking is an addiction. It alters your body chemistry so that you begin to crave cigarettes. Ask anyone who's tried to quit; it's very hard, and most people fail.

- A smoker who gets throat cancer often has his voice box removed. He's called a laryngectomee. A hole, punctured in his neck, goes right to his lungs so he can breathe. Sometimes, even after losing his voice box to cancer, a laryngectomee will continue to smoke. But he doesn't put the cigarette in his mouth anymore. He puts it in the hole in his neck because that's the clearest way to his lungs. If smoking were merely a habit as the tobacco companies insist, a laryngectomee would put the cigarette in his mouth. After all, that's what he's been doing for 20–30 years.

Maribel Bastian,
Nightingale-Bamford School, Manhattan

It was 1953. A research scientist had just established the first strong link between smoking and cancer in an experiment on mice. Concerned, Liggett Group, Inc., quietly decided to duplicate the experiment using its own brands. Cancerous tumors sprouted like mushrooms on the mice's backs. [Yet] Liggett continued to reassure the public that it believed smoking wasn't harmful."

—The Wall Street Journal, *April 4, 1988*

● Consider the fine research being done at the famous Tobacco Institute. They've been researching for years, but darned if they can find any solid evidence that smoking is bad for you.

FIRST SCIENTIST: Well, Ted, for the 13,785th consecutive experiment, all of the cigarette smoking rats developed cancer. What do you make of it?

SECOND SCIENTIST: Beats me, Bob!

FIRST SCIENTIST: It's a puzzle, all right! Hey, look at this—these rats have arranged their food pellets to form the words CIGARETTES CAUSE CANCER YOU ZITBRAINS. What could this possibly mean?

SECOND SCIENTIST: I'm totally stumped, Bob! Back to square one!

—*Dave Barry, Pulitizer Prize-winning columnist*

**Melissa Antonow,
Our Lady of Hope, Queens**

Come to where the Cancer is.

Smoking kills more Americans each year than alcohol, cocaine, crack, heroin, homicide, suicide, car accidents, fires, and AIDS <u>combined</u>.

"Come To Where The Cancer Is" was created in 1989 by Melissa Antonow, a 5th grader, and won best poster in the New York City Smokefree Ad Contest. This ad is being sponsored by the following members of the Coalition For A Smoke-Free City: Alliance For Smoke-Free Air, American Association for Respiratory Care, American Cancer Society, NYC Division, American Council on Science and Health, American Heart Association, NYC Affiliate, American Lung Association of Brooklyn, American Lung Association of Queens, Bedford Stuyvesant Healthy Heart Program, Cancer Care, East Harlem Healthy Heart Program, GASP of New York, Local 1199 Health Care Employees Union, Greater NY March of Dimes, Memorial Sloan-Kettering Cancer Center, New Jersey Commission on Smoking OR Health, New Jersey Group Against Smoking Pollution (GASP), New York County Medical Society, New York Lung Association, NYC Councilman Sal F. Albanese, NYC Department of Consumer Affairs, NYC Department of Health, NYC Health and Hospitals Corporation, Public Health Association of NYC, St. Lukes/Roosevelt Hospital Center, Smokeless Educational Services, and Washington Heights-Inwood Healthy Heart Program. For more information, write to the Coalition For A Smoke-Free City, c/o the NYC Department of Health, 125 Worth Street, Box 46, NYC, NY, 10013 or call (212) 912-0960.

Printing paid for by the Starrett at Spring Creek community
Managed by Grenadier Realty Corp.

> **My uncle hid in a closet to smoke in our house. The clothes caught on fire and our house burned down.**
> —*Fifth-grader from New York*

Cigarette-initiated fires kill 1,500 Americans each year—the equivalent of 10 plane crashes. This makes cigarettes the nation's leading cause of fire deaths in apartments, houses, hotels, motels and mobile homes.

A safer cigarette, one that would go out rather than smolder when left unpuffed, is well within the capability of the tobacco industry and would save hundreds of lives a year. But the industry has rejected such a cigarette for fear fewer might be sold.

Better, the tobacco companies say, to make sofas and mattresses more fire-resistant. (Forests, too?)

- "Ever since a servant mistakenly doused Sir Walter Raleigh with water, believing him to be on fire, smoking has had its opponents. With good reason: the drug Raleigh introduced to Europe now kills about 3 million people a year around the world, and the number is rising fast."
  —The Economist, *September 15, 1990*

**Aggy Swigoniak,
High School of Art and Design, Manhattan**

My name is Patrick Reynolds. My grandfather, R.J. Reynolds, founded the tobacco company that makes Camels, Winstons, and Salems. We've all heard the tobacco industry say there are no ill effects caused by smoking. Well, they ought to look at the R.J. Reynolds family.

"My grandfather chewed tobacco and died of cancer. My father, R.J. Reynolds, Jr., smoked heavily and died of emphysema. My mother smoked and had emphysema and heart disease. My two aunts, also heavy smokers, died of emphysema and cancer. Currently three of my older brothers who smoke have emphysema. I smoked for 10 years and have small-airways lung disease.

"Now tell me. Do you think the cigarette companies are being truthful when they say smoking isn't harmful?"

—*Patrick Reynolds, in a public-service spot prepared by Tony Schwartz*

**Caheim Drake,
P.S. 112, Bronx**

60% of smokers start using cigarettes by the age of 13.

Millions of Americans started smoking to be like Humphrey Bogart, Lucille Ball, John Wayne and the hundreds of other stars who were paid to promote cigarettes. Now history is repeating itself. A whole new generation of young people is becoming addicted to nicotine to be like the stars in movies (most of whom don't smoke in real life). Eddie Murphy's endorsement of king-size Kents in *Beverly Hills Cop* does more to encourage smoking than thousands of magazine ads."

—Tobacco & Youth Reporter, *Autumn 1990*

● In *Lethal Weapon 2*, Mel Gibson smoked in just about every scene where he wasn't killing somebody. Whenever a No Smoking sign was in sight, he made a point of lighting up. Future Mel Gibson movies may be different. Gibson is trying to quit.

**James J. Conte,
Richmond Hill High School, Queens**

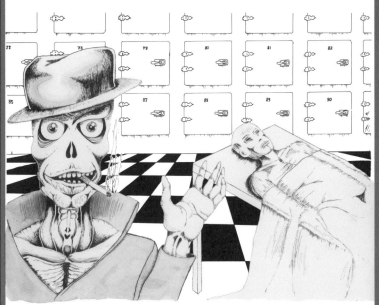

People who are HIV-positive are nearly twice as likely to develop AIDS if they smoke, according to a 56-month study conducted at the University of California at Berkeley of 1,000 HIV-positive men. This stands to reason: tobacco addiction lowers your resistance to disease.

Ismael Zayas,
C.S. 44, Bronx

Things to do instead of smoking

Smell a flower	Make a friend	Pet a Kitty	Tell a Joke

Secondhand smoke is the third leading cause of preventable death in America, after primary smoking and alcoholism.

I t's my life and I want to smoke. I'm not telling you what you should do, so why do you want to tell me what I should do?" We don't want to tell you what you should do. All we're saying is, make sure you know the facts. Then, if you want to smoke, go ahead. But don't do it around others. It's not fair for you to compromise the health of innocent people just because you choose to compromise your own.

• We go to extraordinary expense to remove asbestos from public buildings. Why not remove tobacco smoke as well? It would cost the taxpayer nothing, and it's the greater hazard.

**Lauren Oliva,
P.S. 186, Brooklyn**

The only adults who smoke are children who couldn't quit.

It's as teenagers that most adult smokers become addicted. So what's needed is an effective way to steer teenagers away from smoking. An effective way would be to price cigarettes too high for a kid's pocket. The General Accounting Office estimated that a 20¢ rise in the excise tax on a pack of cigarettes would result in a half-million fewer smokers. Such an increase could also mean a decrease in the number of low birthweight babies born to teenage mothers. Low birthweight, which can have a calamitous, lifelong effect on a child, has been conclusively linked to cigarette use during pregnancy.

"Raising the tax on cigarettes is far more than a way to raise money. It's a way to save lives."

—New York Times, *August 28, 1989*

● The average tax on a pack of cigarettes in Canada is $2.65 vs. just 38¢ in the U.S. This may be why Canadian cigarette sales dropped 30% in the 1980s and a further 9% in the first half of 1990.

**Charlotte Bradley,
P.S. 122, Queens**

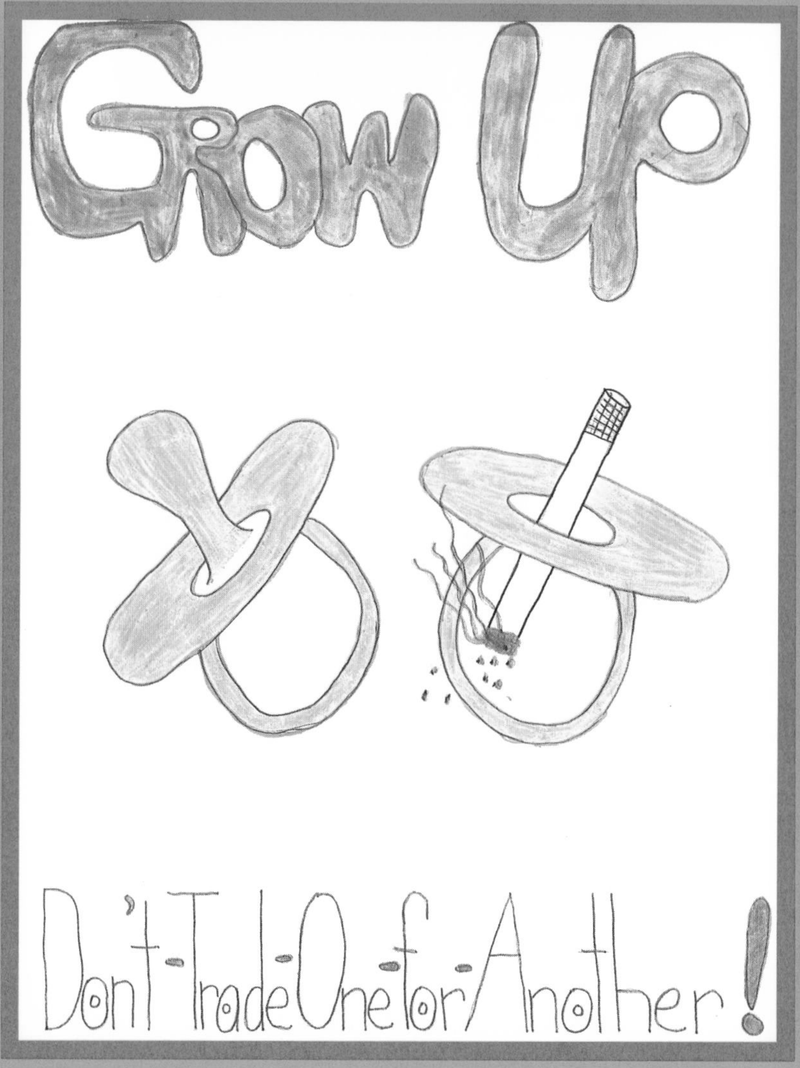
Grow Up
Don't-Trade-One-for-Another!

Kites and notebooks with cigarette logos are distributed free to children in Thailand.

Tobacco companies only warn us about the risks of tobacco addiction because they're forced to. Otherwise, they'd include no warnings. We know this because in countries that don't require health warnings, American tobacco companies provide none.

● In Taiwan, R.J. Reynolds bought out the entire rock concert of local teen idol Hsuow-Yu Chang and made admission "free." All you needed to get in was five empty packs of Winstons.

● The tobacco industry denies that its advertising is designed to hook new smokers or target women. Yet according to an article in *World Watch*, Philip Morris launched Virginia Slims in Hong Kong, amid much fanfare, when only 1% of the women there smoked. Was all that money spent simply to fight for a share of this tiny market?

● More Colombians will die from American tobacco products than Americans will die from Colombian cocaine.

**Juan Morrell,
P.S. 54, Brooklyn**

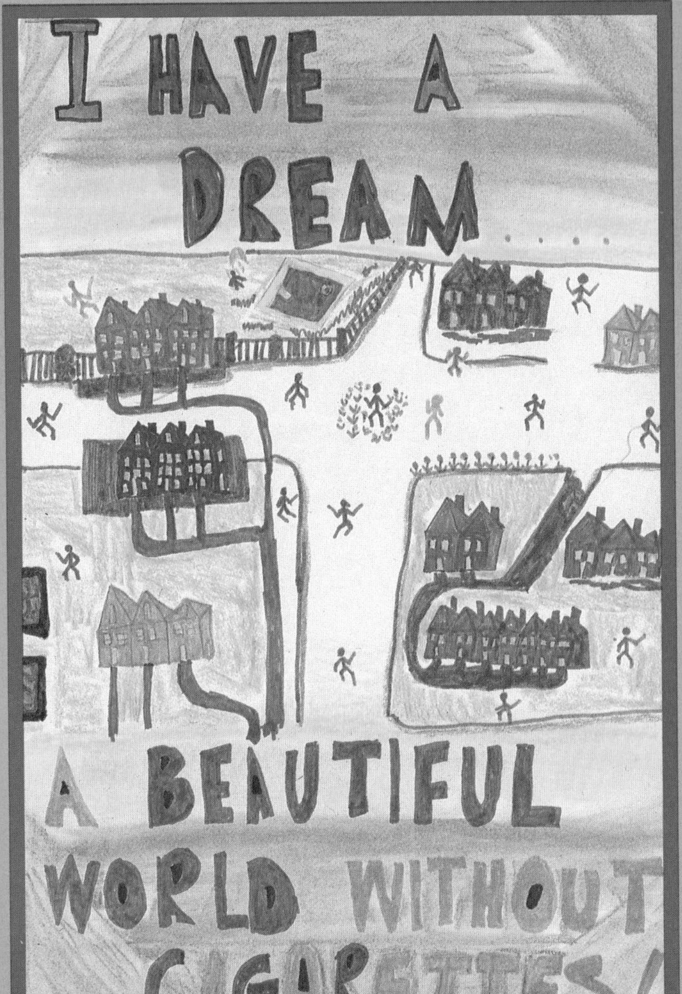
I HAVE A
DREAM....
A BEAUTIFUL
WORLD WITHOUT
CIGARETTES!

In 1990, children under 18 bought cigarettes from vending machines on the order of 450,000 times each day.

My name is Christine Whelan and I am 12 years old. I couldn't testify here today because I had to be in school to take two tests. As part of Mr. Joseph Cherner's cigarette vending machine survey, I went to several Manhattan bars on April 2, 1990, to see if I could buy cigarettes from vending machines without anyone stopping me.

"I was a little nervous the first time I went into a bar because the vending machine was in the center of the room. I walked directly to the machine, which was in plain view of the bartender who was watching me, and purchased cigarettes from the machine. Every time, no one stopped me or tried to talk to me. The only comment was one man saying to the man next to him, 'She's not a regular, she doesn't have holes in her coat.'"

—*From the May 15, 1990, statement of Christine B. Whelan to the New York City Council*

**Cullen Duffy,
Nightingale-Bamford School, Manhattan**

More than 2,500 infant deaths can be attributed to maternal smoking.

A young pregnant smoker was warned by her college professor about the harmful effects of smoking on her unborn child. Hadn't she seen the Surgeon General's warning?

"Oh, don't worry, Professor," she replied quite seriously. "I never buy the packs with that warning on them."

Somehow she thought buying cigarettes with one of the other warnings would spare her fetus.

And do tobacco companies really care? No! Throughout much of the world they're not required to warn pregnant women, so they don't. It might hurt sales.

- Two Swedish doctors, after studying the mothers of 190 infants who died from Sudden Infant Death Syndrome, found that light smokers were twice as likely as smokefree mothers to lose their babies to SIDS and that heavy smokers (10 cigarettes or more a day) were three times as likely. SIDS babies born to smokers lived only two-thirds as long as those born to smokefree mothers.

**Steve Korin,
Mark Twain Jr. High School 239, Brooklyn**

Smokers who haven't been able to quit should keep trying. It usually takes 4 to 10 tries to quit for good.

Within 20 minutes after you quit smoking, blood pressure, pulse rate and body temperature return to normal; within 24 hours, risk of sudden death from heart attack decreases; and within 48 hours, nerve endings in the mouth and nose begin to regenerate. Ex-smokers also tend to experience enhanced self-esteem and an increased sense of control.

- After 15 years off cigarettes, the risk of death returns to nearly normal levels.

**Richard Diaz,
P.S. 20, Queens**

> ## Cancer is a communicable disease. You get it from tobacco companies.

An Oreo boycott was begun against RJR Nabisco because RJR uses cartoon characters in its Camel ads to attract young smokers. Ben & Jerry's joined the boycott in October 1990 by dropping Oreos from its ice cream.

If it seems unfair to boycott a tobacco company's cookie division, note that the idea for linking the two came straight from RJR itself. In 1989 it fired Saatchi & Saatchi, the advertising agency in charge of its Oreo account for 18 years, as punishment for designing Northwest Airlines' smoke-free skies campaign.

- In a *60 Minutes* interview, a Bear Stearns financial analyst called cigarettes a poison disguised as a consumer product. The next day he was fired.

**Craig Perrino,
P.S. 50, Staten Island**

I t seems hard to believe, but the U.S. government, which banned cigarette advertisements on TV, required warning labels on packages and declared through the Surgeon General that tobacco is an addictive drug, is aggressively promoting cigarette use abroad. In Asia, much of the increased smoking has come from U.S. efforts to increase cigarette demand. On Japanese TV, cigarette ads—once rare—now saturate the airwaves, and for the first time are seen during athletic events and programs for children.

Thanks in large part to actions by the U.S. government, a pandemic of lung cancer in Asia is not just likely, it is inevitable."

—Massachusetts Congressman Chet Atkins, January 28, 1989

● "Opium smoking is perfectly innocuous. It is on a par with tea-drinking."

—Attorney for the opium exporters of Hong Kong, 1882

● "Substantial evidence indicates that tobacco is not addictive. The effects of stopping are no different than those experienced upon discontinuance of any other pleasure."

—The U.S. Cigarette Export Association, 1988

Unknown

THESE TWO DO THE SAME THING:

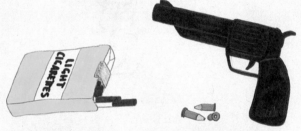

DON'T SMOKE! IT MAY COST YOU YOUR LIFE!

Cigarette advertising shall not suggest that smoking is essential to social prominence, distinction, success or sexual attraction."

—Item #3 of the Tobacco Industry's Principles Covering Cigarette Advertising and Sampling

- In 1990, RJR Nabisco ran a lavish four-page ad for Camels in youth-oriented magazines. It included a coupon for a free pack of Camel cigarettes. "Bored? Lonely? Restless?" ran the headline. "What you need is . . . smooth moves." There followed a pop-up of the appealing "Smooth Character" Camel and three so-called smooth moves: "Foolproof dating advice" (*"Always break the ice by offering her a Camel"*), "How to impress someone at the beach" (*"Always have plenty of Camels ready when the beach party begins"*) and "How to get a FREE pack even if you don't like to redeem coupons" (*"Ask a kind-looking stranger to redeem it"*).

In other words, if you want to get dates, buy Camels. If you want to be included at the beach, buy Camels. If you're too young to buy them, get a kind stranger to buy them for you.

**Luis Lopez,
La Guardia High School, Manhattan**

Smokers should certainly be allowed to increase their own risk of lung cancer and other smoking diseases. No one is suggesting that cigarettes be made illegal. (We tried that: during Prohibition, nine states outlawed tobacco as well as alcohol.) Smokers deserve our sympathy. They are victims.

Likewise, people who grow tobacco or make cigarettes deserve no particular scorn. They are just doing a job in a free economy: supplying demand.

But that special cadre of people who actively try to increase demand are low folk indeed. The marketers, ad executives, lobbyists and lawyers who fight for the right to fly tobacco banners up and down the beach have sold their souls. So, too, the publishers who accept tobacco ads. What they do is legal, but how do they live with themselves?

- It's illegal to sell cigarettes to children in most states. It's illegal to use them in many public places. At best, cigarettes are semi-legal, cancer-causing and addictive.

**Jason Adarno,
C.S. 44, Bronx**

WANTED

For Murder

Description

Mr Cigarette comes in many brands and names. Travels in a pack

Mr Cigarette

crimes:

causes yellow teeth

causes tobacco breath

causes lung Cancer

causes Heart Disease

WARNING: Do not go near him due To Dangers of Secondary Smoke.

Only 26% of Americans still use cigarettes.

Y ou're really the outcast these days if you smoke."
—*Kris M. Schmidt, a Chicago secretary who licked a two-pack-a-day addiction after 15 years, as quoted in* Business Week, *July 27, 1987.*

Lots of people refuse to date smokers. Why limit your options?

- *Dick Gregory:* "Even if I did smoke, I wouldn't do it in front of anybody because I wouldn't want them to know how stupid I was."

- *Dave Barry:* "Today, lighting a cigarette in a restaurant is about as socially acceptable as wandering around spitting into people's salads."

**Sung Joon Han,
Jr. High School 189, Queens**

A model who became known as 'the Winston Man' by appearing in Winston ads for R.J. Reynolds and who smoked three packs a day for 24 years, apologized to school children yesterday for pushing what he called 'the deadliest drug of all.'

" 'The image that I projected is nothing but a bunch of lies made up by ad executives and the tobacco industry,' said David Goerlitz to fifth-grade students at P.S. 63 on Manhattan's Lower East Side.

"Goerlitz, 39, quit smoking last year after visiting his hospitalized, cancer-ridden brother. At the hospital, he met dozens of other cancer patients in their 30s and 40s. Some of them had tubes sticking out of their bodies. Goerlitz asked what could cause so much suffering. The doctors replied, 'Smoking.' "

—New York City Tribune, *February 9, 1989*

● When Goerlitz asked a tobacco company executive why he didn't smoke, the executive replied, "Are you kidding? We reserve that right for the young, the poor, the black, and the stupid."

Frank Cuomo,
Archbishop Molloy High School, Queens

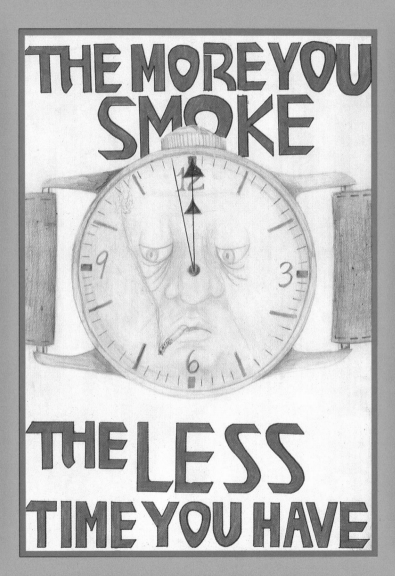

Smokers think lung cancer only happens to someone else. If that were true, it wouldn't happen to anyone.

My grandfather smoked and lived to be 94. And he was never sick a day in his life. What do you say to that?" You could walk blind-folded across the busiest highway in America and possibly not get hurt, but that doesn't make it smart. Only a small percentage who tried would survive. Your grandfather was lucky. But don't forget those around your grandfather. Their health was also being jeopardized, and they may not have been so fortunate. More than 46,000 Americans die each year from secondhand smoke. Smokers risk not only their own health but also the health of those around them.

Joann Acevedo,
P.S. 131, Brooklyn

Do you know that when you smoke.
The smoke gets in your lungs as well
as mine, Please don't smoke Mom and Dad.
I love you too much to see you die,

38% of U.S. businesses are entirely smoke-free.

I'm responsible for overseeing about $1 billion a year, and sometimes I think maybe the fact that I am ruled by this one little thing—cigarettes—means the wrong person is sitting in this chair. Sometimes I think the kid in the stockroom who doesn't smoke is brighter than I am."

—*A health care executive, who requested anonymity, as quoted in the New York* Times, *March 18, 1990*

● Given a choice between a smoker and someone who doesn't smoke, other things being equal, most employers will hire the smoke-free worker.

● A division of Dow Chemical found that smokers averaged 5.5 more days of absence a year than smoke-free employees and 8 more days of disability leave.

**Shyama Patel,
Nightingale-Bamford School, Manhattan**

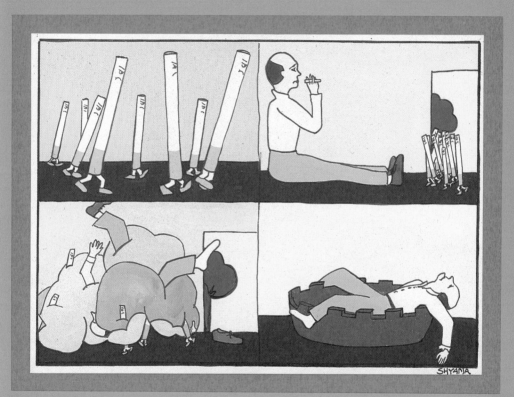

Smoking is cancer country. Are you dying to go there?

My throat was raw. If I touched it, my hand would come away with blood. I was losing weight. I couldn't eat. Everything tasted like mush."
—*Sammy Davis, Jr., on his cancer*

Davis had been a two-pack-a-day man, though this fact was omitted from *People*'s cover story. Tobacco advertising is important to Time Warner, Inc., publishers of *Time, Life, People* and *Fortune*. And if People who smoke have less Time on earth to enjoy Life—well, that's their problem, because by accepting tobacco ads, Time makes a Fortune.

● During the week that *Time* ran a cover story featuring the death of 450 Americans from guns, 8,300 Americans died from smoking. The issue contained ads for Carlton, Marlboro (a two-page spread) and Now (back cover).

Helen Martinez,
Nightingale-Bamford School, Manhattan

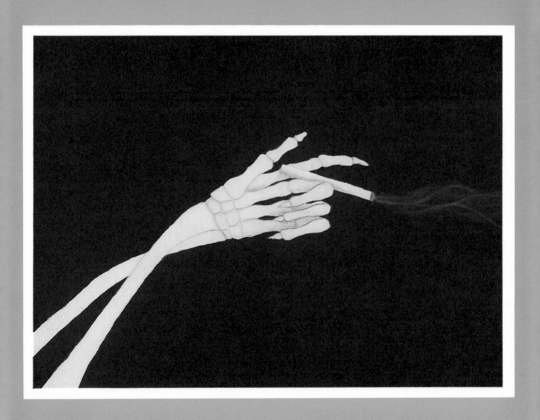

*T*obacco is the principal crop in several congressional districts and a major economic activity in several states. Many people work in the tobacco industry. What about their jobs?" We shouldn't sacrifice the nation's long-term health to avoid short-term unemployment. If 800,000 Americans work in the tobacco industry and 400,000 Americans die each year from smoking, then one American has to die for every two tobacco jobs.

● Did the $8,100 Congressman Edolpus Towns got from the tobacco industry influence his vote against the airline smoking ban? "Not at all," says Towns. "I don't know who contributes to my campaign."

Melissa Ginsberg,
South Shore High School, Brooklyn

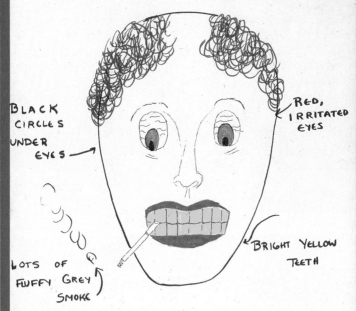

A survey of six large-circulation women's magazines that regularly report on women's health issues found that, from 1983 to 1987, not one of them published a full-length feature, column, review or editorial on *any* aspect of tobacco addiction. During the same five-year period, lung cancer surpassed breast cancer as the number one cancer killer of women. Not one of these magazines [five of which carried tobacco advertising] mentioned it. The survey found 34 articles on breast cancer, but none on lung cancer.

—Wellness Letter, *December 1990*

● In November, 1983 *Newsweek* ran a 16-page special health supplement written by the American Medical Association. Although the original AMA manuscript included information on tobacco addiction, *Newsweek* resisted any mention of cigarettes. That issue of *Newsweek* had 12 full-page cigarette ads.

**Jude Dominique,
Forest Hills High School, Queens**

What used to be suicide is now homicide, too. Second-hand smoke kills people who don't smoke.

In reports and interviews, more than a dozen experts said there was little question that passive smoking caused disease, including lung cancer. What has swayed many scientists is a remarkable consistency in findings from different types of studies in several countries.

"Dr. Stanton A. Glantz of the University of California at San Francisco estimated that passive smoke killed 50,000 Americans a year (as many as died in the entire Vietnam war), two-thirds of whom died of heart disease."

—*New York* Times, *May 29, 1990*

**Emilio Caban,
P.S. 54, Staten Island**

Why do tobacco companies hand out cigarettes at youth-oriented concerts and not at concerts for Frank Sinatra or Mel Torme?

Mark Green, New York City Commissioner of Consumer Affairs: "Fifty years ago, my late father, Irving Green, was handed a free pack of Camels by a tobacco company representative during a break in the middle of a college exam. In his opinion, this one 'gift' got him addicted for half a century."

● Ellen Walker, in *Self-Portrait of a Nicotine Addict* (Hazelden Educational Materials), tells how she became addicted to cigarettes when she was given free packs of Winstons by a fellow college student who got them free in return for passing them out to her friends.

**Tim Windsor,
I.S. 24, Staten Island**

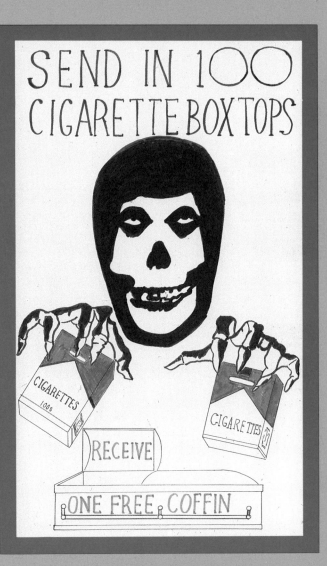

Remember Yul Brynner? Dead from smoking. The man who gave Yul Brynner's eulogy, Alan Jay Lerner? Now dead from smoking. The man who gave Alan Jay Lerner's eulogy, Leonard Bernstein? Dead from smoking. Are you the next link on the smoking chain?"

—Public-service radio spot produced by Tony Schwartz, whose best friend, a policeman, was killed —by lung cancer—at age 47

- Yul Brynner, who starred in *The King and I*, produced his own public-service television spot. "Do I have one piece of advice before I die?" he asked the camera. "Don't smoke."

Alan Jay Lerner co-authored *My Fair Lady*, among other Broadway classics. While he was in the hospital dying of lung cancer, he called his friend Leonard Bernstein nearly every day. "For God's sake, Lenny," he would say to the famous conductor. "Quit! Look what it's done to me."

But Bernstein kept smoking until the day he died. Of lung cancer.

**Jennifer Arena,
P.S. 50, Staten Island**

The cigarette should not be conceived of as a product but as a package....Think of the cigarette pack as a storage container for a day's supply of nicotine.... Think of the cigarette as a dispenser for a dose unit of nicotine."

—*Philip Morris internal research strategy paper*

● Nicotine meets the technical criteria of an addictive drug in laboratory studies by affecting brain wave function, altering mood, and serving as a biological reward that elicits certain behavior from both laboratory animals and human volunteers."

—Science News, *January 18, 1986*

● I was walking home, coughing up more mucus and phlegm than usual. I decided I'd had it. So I crumpled up my pack of cigarettes and threw them in an alley near my home. At three in the morning, I was in the alley on my hands and knees with a flashlight, searching for that pack of cigarettes."

—*David Bresnick, throat cancer victim*

Lily Lin,
Jr. High School 158, Queens

Tobacco—the only product that, when used exactly as the manufacturer intends, causes disease and death.

Tobacco executives claim there's no proof that smoking kills. Yet three major tobacco companies own life insurance companies, and those life insurance companies—like all such companies—charge smokers much higher rates than they charge the rest of us. Why? *Because they know that smokers are nearly twice as likely to die in any given year.*

● American Brands owns both American Tobacco and the Franklin Life Insurance Company; Loews Corporation owns both Lorillard and CNA Life; B.A.T. Industries owns British American Tobacco and Farmers Insurance Group.

● CNA Life recently offered $500,000 of life insurance to 30-year-olds for $425 if they were smoke-free—or $935 if they smoked.

**Tracy Helsing,
St. Stanislaus Kostka School, Brooklyn**

Remember the Perrier benzene scare? It would take 37 bottles of contaminated Perrier to equal the benzene in one pack of cigarettes.

I t's a free country. Why shouldn't people be allowed to smoke?" They should be allowed to—but others shouldn't be forced to breathe their smoke. Cigarette smoke contains, among other things, carbon monoxide, vinyl chloride, hydrogen, cyanide, formaldehyde, and arsenic. Healthy people in the same room with smokers have to breathe these pollutants, too. That's why it's reasonable to ban smoking in public places like elevators, offices, schools, hospitals, buses and airplanes . . . just as we have rules against littering and, well, singing in the library. It's okay to litter your *own* home or sing in your *own* library.

**Mary DiMondo,
South Shore High School, Brooklyn**

Professional women tennis players only push cigarettes. They don't smoke them.

In the six years following the introduction of Virginia Slims cigarettes, the number of teenage girls who smoked regularly more than doubled. The Virginia Slims tennis tournament produced tremendous indirect national TV "advertising," even though cigarette ads have been banned from TV since 1971.

- Angered at Virginia Slims' sponsorship of women's tennis, women doctors protested with placards: "You've Come the Wrong Way, Baby," "Billie Jean Drug King," and "Yes, Virginia, There Is Lung Cancer." This sort of public pressure has forced Virginia Slims to abandon its sponsorship of the women's tennis national tour and to scale back its local tennis sponsorship as well.

- In 1986, lung cancer surpassed breast cancer as the leading cause of cancer death in women.

**Jolanta Pienszykowski,
John Dewey High School, Brooklyn**

THE INVISIBLE TRAP

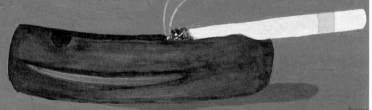

Cigarette companies sell over $1 billion of cigarettes to children each year.

f cigarettes are so bad, why aren't they illegal?" If cigarettes were invented today, they almost surely would be. But by now, with tens of millions of tobacco addicts, it's too late. The good news is: people are catching on.

- In 1976, 28.8% of high school seniors smoked every day. By 1990, that number had dropped to around 16%.

- In the years since the 1964 Surgeon General's Report first announced that smoking causes lung cancer, smoking peaked at 42% of the American adult population. It has been falling ever since, to approximately 26% today.

**José Vega,
P.S. 36, Bronx**

In the fall of 1990, 200 children from Harlem picketed Philip Morris headquarters in New York City, chanting "Thou shalt not kill." They called on Philip Morris to:

- Admit that smoking causes disease
  —90% of lung cancer victims are smokers
  —90% of throat cancer victims are smokers
  —90% of emphysema victims are smokers

- Stop pushing cigarettes on children
  —No more cigarette logos on candy cigarettes
  —No more cigarette billboards near schools
  —No more cigarette billboards at sporting events
  —No more free cigarettes at youth rock concerts
  —No more advertising cigarettes as "athletic" or "sexy"
  —No more paying movies to feature teen heroes smoking

- Stop selling cigarettes without health warnings in under-developed countries.

Philip Morris officials refused to meet with representatives of the demonstrators, who included a priest, a minister and a rabbi.

**Anthony T. Bonamassa,
South Shore High School, Brooklyn**

SMOKING BRINGS YOU NEW FRIENDS

THE CIGARETTE SALESMAN...

THE DOCTOR...

THE MORTICIAN!

Young, growing tissues are much more susceptible to carcinogens than adult tissues are. Bringing up a child in a smoking household is tantamount to bringing him or her up in a house lined with asbestos and radon."
—Dr. William G. Cahan, surgeon at Memorial Sloan-Kettering Cancer Center (who calls his operating room "Marlboro Country")

● *"I'm going to die someday anyway. Why not from smoking?"*
Well, would you rather die peacefully in your sleep one night, of old age, or years earlier, after a long, agonizing illness?

**Nicole Jacques,
I.S. 74, Queens**

The tobacco companies claim their $3 billion in annual advertising and promotion isn't aimed at hooking new smokers, just persuading existing ones to switch brands. If that were true, the industry should favor a total ad ban. Halting all promotion and "freezing" the status quo would increase industry profits by $3 billion annually.

Instead, of course, a prime reason for spending that $3 billion is to attract new addicts: kids.

● "I am always amused by the suggestion that advertising, a function that has been shown to increase consumption of virtually every other product, somehow miraculously fails to work for tobacco products."

—*Emerson Foote, former chairman of McCann-Erickson, one of the world's largest ad agencies*

**Lisa Karen Prusnofsky,
Abraham Lincoln High School, Brooklyn**

IF YOU SMOKE

THE JOKE
IS ON YOU

Liggett paid $30,000 to feature Eve cigarettes in *Supergirl*.

I n 50 years of Superman comics, Lois Lane never smoked; then Philip Morris paid $42,500 to feature Marlboro ads in Superman movies, and she began chain-smoking Marlboro Lights. It's hard to find a movie that *doesn't* advertise cigarettes or glamorize tobacco addiction. In fact, the National Coalition on Television Violence reviewed 133 films between July 1987 and June 1988 and found smoking in 87% of those rated PG.

• Philip Morris paid $350,000 to get James Bond to smoke Larks in *Licence to Kill*.

• In *Who Framed Roger Rabbit,* detective Eddie Valiant is offered Lucky Strikes by a teenager. A Lucky Strike billboard appears prominently several times as well. Coincidence?

Alan Goldstein,
South Shore High School, Brooklyn

VERY IMPORTANT, PLEASE READ CAREFULLY!!!
I need all of you [to denote] stores that are heavily frequented by young adult shoppers. These stores can be in close proximity to colleges, high schools, or areas where there are a large number of young adults."
—*J.P. McMahon, Division Manager,*
in a January 10, 1990, memo to R.J. Reynolds sales reps

● In 1990 R.J. Reynolds launched Dakota cigarettes, targeted at girls under 21 with little education, who hold low-level jobs, and who attend drag races and tractor pulls with their boyfriends.

● "The simple and unfortunate fact is that scientists do not know the cause or causes of the chronic diseases reported to be associated with smoking. More scientific research is needed."
—*Response from R.J. Reynolds to a fifth-grade class in Amherst,*
New York, who wrote about RJR's brand names on children's toys

Amarilys Candelaria,
P.S. 124, Brooklyn

In response to mounting criticism, the Tobacco Institute at the end of 1990 introduced a brochure called "Tobacco: Helping Youth Say No." But, says Joe Cherner, president of Smokefree Educational Services, "Nowhere in the booklet do you see the words *cancer* or *heart disease*. Nowhere is there mention of the fact that smoking is addictive and can kill you. Only the tired old mantra that smoking is an adult custom, like driving a car or getting married. That's not a disincentive for children. On the contrary, most children start smoking to seem more adult. The industry's most effective advertising is to convince kids that smoking is adult and grown-up."

● As much as parents and teachers would like to see their children smoke-free, the only people who can make that decision are the children themselves. We must give them enough information to choose intelligently.

Ravi Blank,
Abraham Lincoln High School, Brooklyn

CIGARETTES

HARMLESS

UNTIL

YOU USE THEM

A team led by Charles Chittenden analyzed data on 1,807 adult males, of whom 1,375 had been lifetime smokers. The rest had never smoked. The study found that a 30-year-old smoker could expect to live another 34.8 years, compared with another 52.7 years for a 30-year-old who'd never smoked—a difference of 17.9 years!*

● But it's even worse, because the last few years of a smoker's life often involve surgical removal of a lung, or the tongue or larynx. Newport's slogan, "Alive with Pleasure," strikes your average chemotherapy patient, wracked with nausea, as somehow . . . inappropriate.

*Their findings are reported in the May/June 1990 issue of *Contingencies*, the journal of the American Academy of Actuaries.

Vicki Man,
High School of Fashion Industries, Manhattan

Tobacco advertising is banned from Olympic sports facilities.

In the late 1960s, tobacco executives crossed their hearts and hoped to die if they ever showed another athlete in a cigarette ad. Since then, through signs located in key TV angles at sports stadiums, tobacco companies have found a less expensive way to juxtapose their cigarette brands with athletes.

"Fourteen major league baseball stadiums in the U.S. have giant billboards for Marlboro; eight carry signs for Winston. Only Wrigley Field and Dodger Stadium offer the chance to watch a game without a macho dope from a cigarette company looking over the outfield fence.

"Auto racing is a nonstop cigarette commercial. Reviewing a videotape of the 1989 Marlboro Grand Prix on NBC, I counted 5,992 visual and verbal mentions of the cigarette brand name and logo in the 90-minute telecast."

—Dr. Alan Blum, family physician and founder of DOC: Doctors Ought to Care

**Allen Chong,
P.S. 222, Brooklyn**

Laurence Tisch, president of CBS, and his brother Preston, the former Postmaster General, have donated $30 million to New York University Hospital, which is to be renamed Tisch Hospital. The Tisch brothers make the bulk of their money from Lorillard, a tobacco company that sells such popular brands as Newport, Kent and True. The Surgeon General reports that more than 434,000 Americans die each year from smoking, so the Tisch brothers are doing something really unprecedented in the annals of medical philanthropy—providing both the hospitals and the patients."

 —*Larry White, author of* Merchants of Death:
  The American Tobacco Industry

• "A prominent heart surgeon told me that if everyone stopped smoking today, more than one-third of all the hospitals in this country would close in the next five years."

 —*Larry King,* USA Today

**Mairut Luu,
P.S. 33, Bronx**

Keep The Hospitals Empty! DON'T SMOKE!

> **You won't send flowers to my funeral, will you, Philip Morris? I didn't think so.**
> —*Mike Royko*

I have a particular reason for disapproving of smoking. My late brother, David Millar, died of emphysema complications caused by smoking. He was, ironically, the first Marlboro Man. The death notice in the school bulletin where we both attended listed my brother's cause of death as smoking. I hope that makes an impression."

—*the late Marlboro Man's sister*

● Hamish Maxwell, chairman of Philip Morris, maker of Marlboros, told interviewers for years that smoking hadn't been proven to cause any harm. In 1990, Maxwell, a heavy smoker, underwent quadruple bypass surgery. We haven't seen Mr. Maxwell smoking since.

**Adriana Villanueva,
High School of Fashion Industries, Manhattan**

In 1991, the Oakland A's became the first major league baseball team to ban smoking in their stadium.

Spitting used to be common practice in restaurants. There were spittoons beside each table. You'd be eating, and someone at the next table would be spitting. If you did this in a restaurant today, you'd probably be thrown out. (And spitting doesn't give anyone cancer.) Just as it's hard to imagine how our grandparents permitted spitting in restaurants, it's going to be hard for our grandchildren to understand how we allowed smoking in restaurants—or any other enclosed public space.

**Anandi Premlall,
P.S. 55, Queens**

> **"Smoking is a custom loath-
> some to the eye, hateful to the
> nose, harmful to the brain,
> and dangerous to the lungs."**
> —*King James I, 1604*

"*Forty? Fifty? Sixty? By the time I'm that old, they'll have found a cure for lung cancer. Anyway, that's a million years from now. I'll never live that long.*" Sure you will. And when you do, a year will be just as precious to you as it is today—maybe even more so, because by then you'll have your own car and *no homework*.

**Dahlia Scheindlin,
Midwood High School, Brooklyn**

THE END

ORGANIZATIONS OF INTEREST

Pro-health Groups

The Advocacy Institute
1730 Rhode Island Ave., NW
Washington, DC 20036

American Cancer Society
1599 Clifton Rd., NE
Atlanta, GA 30322

American Heart Association
7320 Greenville Ave.
Dallas, TX 75231

American Lung Association
1740 Broadway
New York, NY 10019

Americans for Nonsmokers' Rights
2530 San Pablo Ave.
Berkeley, CA 94702

ASH: Action on Smoking and Health
2013 H St., NW
Washington, DC 20006

DOC: Doctors Ought to Care
1423 Harper St.
Augusta, GA 30912

Smokefree Educational Services, Inc.
375 South End Ave., #32F
New York, NY 10280

STAT: Stop Teenage Addiction to Tobacco
121 Lyman St. #210
Springfield, MA 01103
Publishes *Tobacco and Youth Reporter*

Tobacco groups

Smoker's Advocate
800-343-0975. This is actually a Philip Morris phone number. They will send free newsletters and the Philip Morris magazine.

Smoker's Caucus
800-222-5995. Another Philip Morris phone number. They send anti-health information to enlist support for stopping pro-health legislation.

Smokers's Rights Alliance
800-562-7444. Although they claim to receive no help from the tobacco industry, sometimes the operator mistakenly answers "Nelson, Ralston, Robb"—the PR firm for the Tobacco Institute.

Tobacco Action Network
800-424-9876. This is actually the phone number for the Tobacco Institute.

Smokers' Rights Action Line
800-333-8683. An R.J. Reynolds phone number.